The 5 Decisions Big Dreamers Make Before Their Franceformation
Copyright © 2019-2020 by Allison Grant Lounes.

All rights reserved. No part of this publication may be reproduced, distributed, or transmitted in any form or by any means, including photocopying, recording, or other electronic or mechanical methods, without the prior written permission of the publisher, except in the case of brief quotations embodied in critical reviews and certain other noncommercial uses permitted by copyright law. For permission requests, write to the publisher at the address below.

Allison Grant Lounes
www.yourfranceformation.com
welcometo@yourfranceformation.com

Ordering Information:
Quantity sales. Special discounts are available on quantity purchases by corporations, associations, and others. For details, contact the author at the address above.

Introduction

If you want to move to France, and you want to create a completely new life for yourself, it's not just because you have a dream. It's because you are a dreamer at heart. It takes a brave person, and a creative person, to imagine something so completely different from your current life and to consider the steps you would need to manifest these profound changes to what you've always known. I know, because if you are reading this book, we have quite a bit in common.

Let's face it. As much as some aspects of French politics or society may appeal to you, you don't move to a new country for universal healthcare, you move because you want the freedom of pursuing your art or music without the burden of fearing that breaking your arm or getting into a minor car accident will bankrupt you. Aspiring to move to France - for several years, or permanently - rather than simply travel there, means that deep down, some part of you feels like you'll feel more at home, or more yourself, when you live in France. You believe it will make you happy, or bring you peace, enabling you to live the life you envision for yourself in a way that your current location can't.

The sense of longing you feel for the life you want to create is normal, because it is in our nature as humans to grow, and expand, and seek new experiences, and to create the lives we desire. Part of being human, and being alive, is wanting to create something more and better for ourselves and our families.

When you dream of moving to France, I know you're not just dreaming of living in a place where you can eat a crêpe au Nutella while walking down the street, casually stop for a glass of wine at the terrasse of your neighborhood café after work, or go to a museum any time you want, although those are all significant advantages. You may dream of travel, of universal health insurance, or of various aspects of French culture, but often, what you truly want, is your ability to be more yourself. You move because of the feelings you want to have and experience when you create this new life. You move to let go of the baggage and disappointments of how your current life doesn't meet the expectations you set for yourself, and you get the opportunity to begin anew, leaving behind everything from your old life that no longer serves you.

Maybe you want to begin a new challenge or start a new adventure. If your current life - job, and town, and the humdrum of your daily activities - no longer excites or invigorates you, you may be anticipating that the challenges of traveling, settling in a new country, conquering the bureaucracy, and discovering new activities in a new language will stimulate your mind and your senses, expand your horizons, and breathe new life into your creative spirit. Maybe you feel like your opportunities are limited, and grieve a place you feel like you no longer belong.

France is a place that inspires art with the beauty of its public spaces, but also a place that leaves space for art to grow outside of the consume-or-be-consumed culture of capitalism. If what we desire is to be inspired, to expand our intellectual pursuits, to challenge ourselves outside of our pursuit of money-making, to make art, to write our stories, to be spiritually and emotionally fulfilled, to pursue creative expression in any of its forms, it's only natural that France would be the place we'd want to make that happen. Americans in particular have always seen France through rosy glasses. When good Americans die, as Audrey Hepburn once said, we go to Paris. Some of the greatest American artists, writers, and philosophers of the early 20th century spent time meandering along the banks of the Seine and participating in the rich intellectual and cultural life the city has to offer. Countless writers and artists still are inspired by the magnificence of everything from the old Haussmannian architecture to the older medieval castles in the Loire valley.

Because you are deciding to move to France, and you are reading this book, I know you already possess certain qualities that will serve you well during your Franceformation.

You are brave.

Best-selling author and professor of social work Dr. Brené Brown says, "Vulnerability is not about losing. It is about showing up when you can't control the outcome." And by reading this book or having a dream as big as moving to another country, you are being incredibly brave. While you may have ideas and dreams about how you want your life and your move to turn out, you know that you can't control what your life may look like once you arrive in France. You can't control whether you get the visa or job you want, or what the conditions will be if and when you arrive in France and begin to build a new life. Dreaming big means accepting the possibility that things won't work out the way you'd like, and taking even the smallest steps to pursue those dreams shows vulnerability and bravery. You should feel proud of yourself that you are undertaking a project that many people are not willing or able to see through to the end.

You are open-minded.

When we we are open-minded, we are aligned with the energy of solutions, rather than the energy of problems. We are willing to ask questions and consider endless options, and we remain open to the possibility that our first choice, or first thoughts, may not be the best ones in the long-term.

One of the major causes of failure I see, when people plan to move abroad but never seem to make it come to fruition, is that they become fixated on one particular way to make it work: one particular type of job, or one particular path, or one specific opportunity, and their attachment to that outcome prevents them from seriously considering other solutions. Sometimes, they persist in rejecting all other outcomes, even when there are ways to make their move happen, because they are unable to consider the possibilities. By reading this book and exploring the possibilities, you increase your chances of making your move a success and of effecting long-term change.

You are curious.

People who are not curious don't want to move to other countries, or learn new languages. They don't want to confront the challenges of living in a new culture or adapting to a new way of life. They avoid stepping out of their comfort zone and learn how to do things in a new way.

Curiosity about yourself and others is a gift that will enable you to continually grow and evolve as a human, and which will allow you to create meaningful connections with people across cultural and linguistic barriers. As you develop your plan and proceed with creating your dream life, please stay curious about what you want and *why* you want it, because your awareness will help you to enjoy the creation process.

You have grit.

Grit is passion and sustained persistence applied toward long-term achievement, and anyone who undertakes an international move and navigates a career change in a new language definitely has it. To make this move happen, you are going to have to evaluate every aspect of your life, and do a lot of tasks that are boring, uncomfortable, frustrating, or seemingly have no purpose. Sometimes, the French bureaucracy you will encounter will make no sense, and its purpose won't be clear, and you'll think that there must be an easier or more effective way. You will question why you even want whatever it is you want. You may want to give up.

It's normal to go through periods of frustration, or culture shock, or even depression and doubt as you move through the process and navigate French administration. Having assistance and guidance along the way will help, but it may not mitigate those feelings entirely. Your ability to stay the course despite bureaucracy fatigue or emotional exhaustion will depend on your determination to exercise your grit muscle and have faith in the life you are creating for yourself.

You are committed to growing and to learning new things.

It is impossible to want to move to a new country without anticipating growth and expansion in all areas of your life. And that's exciting! No matter what your language skills are currently, or where you feel you may not be "ready," you can begin, right where you are at this moment, and get ready to get ready. Growth and change don't happen all at once, and there probably won't be any one defining moment you can point to as your moment of readiness. By embarking on this journey, you are signaling your readiness for personal growth and evolution as you become the person who makes your dreams come true.

And most importantly, you have big dreams that you want to turn into plans and goals.

Do you know what the difference is between a dream and a goal? A dream becomes a goal when you set a deadline for it and begin taking action towards achieving it. In other words, a dream plus a plan becomes an achievable goal. Sometimes, the path or the plan to the goal isn't entirely clear, but that doesn't mean it's impossible. It just means you need to create clarity as you take small, consistent action to defining your dream and bringing it to life.

Many others have come before you, and many others are embarking on the same journey as you, right now. Some will succeed and create their new life in France, while others will not. I want *you* to be among those who are able to bring their dreams to life, and throughout this book, I'm going to give you guidance on how to ensure that you maximize your chances of joining this group.

You don't have to be special or smart or have any qualities in particular to make your dreams come true. You are already worthy, just as you are, and, as part of the process, we will make sure you're qualified (visa-wise). You just need belief in yourself, and determination, and the open-mindedness to make it happen.

I have guided many of those who have come before you, and I'm here to show you the way forward, too. And as with many of my clients, I'm here to guide you along the path, point out the pitfalls and the hazards along the way, and help you to stay on track while you enjoy the scenery and the journey. Let's explore the decisions you'll need to make before you embark on your Franceformation and the actions you'll need to take to ensure that it's a success.

Before we get started: a note, in case you're wondering: what is a "Franceformation"?

In another life, my business was called Paris Unraveled. A late friend from my choir found the name, based on the idea of unraveling the mysteries of French bureaucracy and administration, and of living in Paris. While I loved the name for several years, I started to feel like I was growing out of it. For one thing, I had inquiries from people who thought I *only* worked with people moving to Paris, and I constantly had to clarify that my clients were from all over the world and moving to all different regions of France. And I began to dislike the imagery of the word "unraveled," which depicts something falling apart. While your life may unravel as you begin to transform - there's always a breakdown before a breakthrough - "unraveling" can be a scary image rather than a positive vision of the new life you'll create.

When I was revising and renaming my service packages and my business in late 2019, I also began to acknowledge that the work I was doing wasn't just providing visa support and a completed visa application. In fact, one of the main components of the service I was providing was emotional support and coaching through my client's periods of doubt that their move would happen. And my clients wanted to feel like they were supported throughout the entire process, from conception through the "fourth trimester," or the magical period after arriving in France but before they are truly established and feeling secure. My job wasn't just about providing information and delivering the finished application, it was to be a midwife to this new life and to support them on the emotional journey they sometimes weren't prepared for as we created it together.

The concept of Franceformation ties in a few different ideas. The transformation of my client's lives, in all of the most practical ways through the emotional transformation that accompanies major life changes such as an international move. In English, the word "formation" is the creation of something new, or it can represent an orderly or organized structure. In French, the word "formation" is a training or educational program, and a Franceformation encompasses a period of learning about yourself, your dreams, and your abilities, along with more broad topics like living in France, the French visa and renewal process, and various French bureaucracy and administration. It also includes learning new language skills and adapting to a new culture and way of life. Finally, a formation is also a deposit of solid rock, which represents the solid foundation we create for the projects and life goals my clients develop.

Franceformation, / fræns fɔrˈmeɪ ʃən /, n.f.:

1. The creation of one's new life in France;

2. The personal transformation one undergoes when moving to France and incubating a new life;

3. The intense period of learning about oneself, about French bureaucracy, and about French language and culture, which occurs as one prepares to move to France and adapts to a new culture;

4. A full-service and support program to nurture you from the moment you decide to move to France, through your visa application, arrival, and beyond.

Are you ready to commit to yours?

Big Dreamers decide to move to France and commit despite knowing about the challenges.

When you begin to seriously consider the possibility of moving to France, of asking yourself whether this idea is something you may actually want to create for yourself, you'll immediately have many questions on exactly how to make it work.

Is it possible to move to France, in my current or future circumstances?

Am I willing to commit to moving to France and make the decision to move forward? Do I really want it enough to put in the effort?

Once I've decided I want to, what are the pitfalls and challenges along the way? Will it work out? Am I emotionally resilient enough to see the challenges and work through them, or am I emotionally fragile in ways that will inhibit my success?

The research brings up all kinds of challenges, frustrations, and obstacles to moving, because immigration is hard and I will have to learn and adapt to many new situations. Will I be able to overcome the issues?

Will the move to France be as good as I think it will be, or will I be disappointed and frustrated?

You're reading this book because somewhere, germinating in your mind, is the idea that you want something different, and you're considering that maybe, moving to France is the right 'something different' to change your life.

Maybe you have paid your dues, finished a corporate career to a solid retirement, and want to go off on a new adventure and learn a new language and immerse yourself in a slower way of life. Maybe you're at the beginning of your career, wondering if all you have to look forward to over the next 40 or 50 years is a couple weeks of vacation spread out here and there, and the occasional longer trip abroad. Maybe you're tired of the rat race of American culture of working 75 hours a week 52 weeks a year and enamored with places that have universal healthcare that bankrupts nobody, and schools where nobody ever gets shot.

Whatever your situation, you've wondered if there's more. If it would be possible to live in one of those old European cities you've visited and fell in love with, and what that would mean for your life and your career. You know in your heart that it must be possible – that other people do it, move abroad and become expats, but maybe you've never imagined that it could be you.

You've just hoped.

And you're reading this book because you want to find out if it could truly be possible for you. The idea of leaving behind your current life situation for a new adventure abroad excites and invigorates you, but you have no idea where to start. The stakes are high: it's your life, after all, but reading this book is a tiny step towards discovering what else is out there for you. Whether living abroad – living in France – is a passing fancy for you, or whether you've thought about it for years, you are beginning to wonder how to stop dreaming and start actually planning to make it happen.

The truth is that it's hard to invest your time and energy and sometimes money in a big dream that may not work out, or when you don't see exactly how you can make it happen. As long as moving to France stays in the realm of "dream" or "something I'd like to do one day," it is a thing that can bring you daydreams and excitement, but not pain or stress. When something is merely a daydream, before it is a plan, you don't have to figure out your whole life around it and make changes that may be difficult or painful. You can develop enough of an emotional attachment to the idea to feel the pleasure of thinking about it, without the threat and pain of loss if working on a move doesn't work out or isn't as satisfying as you'd like it to be.

Ultimately, though, having unfulfilled dreams and desires and life experiences stack up around you because you don't know if you'll be able to make them possible can take a toll, as you begin to wonder whether you're living to pay the bills and get by in your current life, or whether you truly have the opportunity to live the life you want. You start to doubt whether you get to create the experiences you want. And you question whether you and your dreams are worthy enough to fulfil.

As your viewpoint evolves from "moving to France would be nice" to "I want to move to France within the next couple of years," or even "I'm ready to begin the process of moving to France now," the research and the details of what you'll have to do can almost immediately bog you down and discourage you. The emotional mismatch between your lofty, imaginative goals for yourself and the confusion or the frustrating bureaucratic minutia of actually getting it done can seem overwhelming, especially if you receive conflicting or argumentative advice online or are on the receiving end of doubt and negativity. Focusing on the questions of how you'll sort through all of the conflicting advice and how you'll get from where you are now to where you want to be forces you outside of your comfort zone. And when you are in the space where doubt and the discomfort of your unresolved questions are bigger and more present than your dream: that's where you are most likely to give it up.

You think you're going to have to compromise on things that are important to you, or being pigeon-holed in your career or your opportunities, because of your immigration status or ability to speak French.

You worry that you won't be able to do what you REALLY want to do in France - whatever that is - and that visa restrictions will stunt your personal or professional development and prevent you from creating the path you want to follow.

You fret about making the wrong decision, choosing the wrong visa, or the wrong job, or maybe none of the options feels exactly right for you because you don't know what they would look like or how you might make them work financially.

Some of the challenges you'll potentially face during the move, like the professional development identity crisis, or the endless apartment search, are predictable. Even if certain challenges are not totally avoidable, my clients find that having someone to help them anticipate and navigate various situations enables them to regulate their emotional responses to issues that may otherwise cause them despair. Blessed with passion and enthusiasm for projects they undertake, big dreamers are often attached to the outcome of the visa application and to the ideal life they've dreamed of and are sometimes too close to the situation to reevaluate and respond.

A client of mine, Julie, received an email from the French embassy after submitting her visa application, requesting additional documents showing her financial resources and bank accounts, and she emailed me in a tizzy, concerned that her application was incomplete and that her pre-move income wouldn't be sufficient for the visa. After considering how best to reassure her, I replied: "This is great news. It means your visa application and business plan have been approved, and they're ready to give you your visa. They just need this final document to check off all of their boxes, and you'll have your visa in no time." Flipping the switch on a stressful what-if-it's-not-good-enough train of thought and explaining what's on the other side of the request, and how things really work behind the scenes in French administration, can take the worry and the uncertainty out of these interactions.

Your internal stress voice, the one that can ramp up your anxiety or reassure you depending on its mood on any given day, doesn't *know* in this situation whether or not everything will be fine. With experience and an understanding of The Way Things Work Here, you may need to develop the internal voice of Every Little Thing Is Gonna Be Alright.

Sometimes, the reason you may be considering working with me on your move to France is because you've *already* tried to make it happen on your own, and haven't been able to make it work. I have met with people who submitted dozens, if not hundreds, of job applications to French companies before realizing that with their credentials, the chances of them being sponsored were slim to none. I have met with people who pursued a temporary visa path, like a student visa for language courses, or a visitor visa while they planned to seek employment, only to realize they had gotten themselves into a bit of a mess, because there was no easy way out of the visa path they were on so they could do what they actually wanted to do.

When this happens — when, despite their best efforts, someone hasn't been able to make it work in the past — it is easy to lose faith and to begin to believe that what they want isn't meant to be. It can take time to process past missteps and mistakes and to feel truly confident that things are working out for the best, and that it's still possible to create the life they want to create in France. Delays or deferments, in the world of French bureaucracy, are not necessarily a "non." Sometimes, it's just the processing time for the paperwork in the great cosmic bureaucracy.

As I write this book, France, and most of the world, is in confinement from Covid-19, and we are ending our first month of lockdown and going into a second month. Many of my clients are in limbo, having begun the visa application process and prepared to move, only to be confronted with visa offices that are closed and application processing that has been suspended indefinitely. One of my clients has her visa in hand, but cannot board a flight; another client's passport is sitting in the French Embassy in Washington, DC, pending approval, and she likely won't receive it back until the situation becomes more clear. This is a challenge and a delay none of us could have predicted when we began working together in December. And we anticipate that once the borders *do* open up again, we will be confronted with backlogged appointments, slow processing, and a hesitation to travel and risk spreading disease again.

But these challenges, even big, seemingly insurmountable challenges like a global pandemic, are temporary. They are not tests about how serious you are, nor are they signs that you shouldn't do the thing you've been dreaming of or planning for so long. They are not moral lessons, and they're not personal frustrations. They are not even challenges to your dream itself.

These challenges ask you, over and over, an important question: who do you want to be while you are bringing your dream to life? What will you do, and who do you want to be, while you are waiting?

Do you want to be someone who is positive, and patient, and tries to identify solutions? Do you want to be someone who asks for help, and who figures out how to make things work?

Or do you want to be the person who gives up, because the frustrations and emotional dips that accompany the realization of your dream are too much to handle?

Do you want your dream to enable you to grow, or cause you to shrink?

With assistance, grit, and time, there are very few relocation challenges that can't be overcome but anticipating them and planning for them can help you to navigate your move more easily.

Jackie was a project manager in New England who dreamt of moving to France, but her passion wasn't project management. It was wine. Although she had studied oenology in prestigious programs in Europe and in the US, virtually all of her experience was merely for fun. She had never worked in the wine industry, nor had she had any formal work experience in a related field.

What she lacked in formal experience and confidence, she

made up with passion and enthusiasm, and she was committed to making her move happen from our very first call. As we worked together and discussed the best way for her to bring her dream of living in France to life, we hotly debated the two main possibilities. We could either put together a dull but solid application for her to be a freelance project manager, which would enable her to continue her existing projects while working virtually and to find clients in Europe who needed a bilingual team member. Or, she could take the leap into pursuing her passion, and put together a proposal for a wine-based business.

After going back and forth several times on the premise of her project proposal, Jackie ultimately decided that she was committed to using the opportunity of her move to France to create something totally new and different for herself, including a job she was excited and passionate about. She understood that she'd be facing not only the administrative challenges of moving to France, but also of figuring out how to set the course and navigate her new chosen career path. Embarking on a brand-new business idea outside of her comfort zone, as part of an international move, was a major leap of faith. She knew she'd have to build her business idea and have some income during the first year in order to be able to renew her visa, so we needed to create a solid action plan.

As we developed the business plan, I explained the other challenges that we would face together as we established the business. She'd have to register multiple business activities, including a reselling activity, and get the appropriate licenses for the wine she'd provide to her customers. We developed several aspects of the business, from reselling wine from small local producers, to wine tours, to gift baskets including wine that small businesses and AirBnbs could provide to their guests or customers. The logistics of developing her business would be complex, but it enabled her to forge relationships with French wineries, to try lots of different wines, and to share that love of locally produced French wines with tourists and other French businesses.

When her visa was approved and it came time to actually register the business in Paris, there were challenges galore. We went to the préfecture's alcohol licensing bureau several times to get the right forms filed and to understand the regulations. We created the business registration for both a tourism and tour activity, and for a wine reselling activity. We double- and triple-checked the regulations to ensure that the ways in which she wanted to serve her clients (providing picnic baskets with wine and doing wine tours and tastings) were authorized. And she began to find clients for her fledgling business.

For this particular business type and project, there were lots of moving parts and authorizations she needed in order to be able to operate the business legally and successfully. Jackie knew she'd face many challenges while creating her new business in a different industry, and understood that there was a potentially overwhelming number of administrative tasks involved with the type of business she wanted to operate. But, her passion for her project and her eagerness to prove herself enabled her to get a visa and to start strong.

Big Dreamers decide that pursuing their dreams is an important and worthy mission.

I believe, without hesitation, that the following statements are true:

- Pursuing your dreams and following your desire are important to you. It gives meaning, purpose, and direction to your life, and you are worthy and deserving of pursuing your dreams regardless of who you are and of what they are, and regardless of whatever mistakes you have made in the past.

- Pursuing your dreams and your passion projects is important to the world, because people who pursue their dreams and goals become better people and make important contributions to humanity.

- Pursuing your dreams makes you grow and evolve as a person. It makes you a better, more highly motivated, more open-minded and successful person.

- The world needs more people with a globalized perspective, and people who are wiling to put in the effort to understand other languages and cultures.

Cultivating such skills results in more people who are empathetic, thoughtful, and able to see problems and solutions from multiple perspectives.

- In a globalized world, the abilities to move freely and to speak multiple languages are assets and gifts. We are especially sensitive to that now that COVID has closed borders, separated families, stranded people all over the world, and brought travel to a grinding halt. Our ability to connect across languages and cultures makes the world a better place.

Your dreams are important. Your life is important. You only get one life, but you can have and pursue many dreams. And once you have a dream about something as big as living in France, the magnitude of the dream can begin to shed light onto the stuckness you may be feeling about your ability to Do Big Things.

The topic becomes two subjects – wanting to move abroad, and your perceived stumbling blocks to moving abroad. Your uncertainty about exactly how you will make it happen – what visa you'll get, what job you'll get, if your skills enable you to get a job or a sponsored visa — can foster doubt. And the more you ruminate on the topic, wondering how you could make a move happen, the more it reveals the discomfort and stagnation you feel where you currently are. The more you doubt your ability to move to France and to create the life you desire as part of your relocation, the more you'll doubt your inherent worthiness to pursue *any* of your dreams.

Your dreams, and the things you generally want out of life, may include many things, both in terms of what you want to accomplish and the type of lifestyle or environment you want to have.

You may dream of having a secure position in your dream job earning a good living salary, working remotely, or freelancing/running a small business that enables you to work from home with clients from anywhere in the world.

You may dream of having a confident mindset that allows you to follow your heart and your interests without resistance.

You may dream of having the right visa that enables you to develop professionally in the way you want, and to renew, change statuses, or eventually apply for residency or naturalization in France.

You may dream of living in a place where you have access to universal healthcare, or where there are no school shootings and little gun violence.

You may dream of a calmer, more relaxed way of life that takes you outside of the rat race of corporatism, with 25+ vacation days and 12 paid holidays per year, mandatory overtime pay, instead of giving your life away to companies for a pittance.

You may dream of the ability to travel in Europe easily, and having a path to a second passport.

You may simply dream of learning French, walking along the Seine, drinking wine from Bordeaux that costs €4 in the supermarket, eating a baguette and trying 400 different kinds of cheese.

It doesn't matter what your dreams are or why you want them. What matters are your feelings about them and about the person you want to become. You've made the commitment in your heart to move - but your knowledge about how to do that and your confidence in your ability to make it happen need to catch up, and you need to make it happen without sabotaging yourself.

It isn't my job - or anyone's job - to judge the worthiness of you or of your dreams, or how those dreams fit into the work you want to do on Earth as a person and as a soul to grow and evolve. Your dream could be to work for a multinational company and travel all over on business, or to write a book of poetry, or to make beautiful art or music to share with others, or to have a quiet life surrounded by family and close friends. Your dreams are up to you. And because they are your dreams, they are worthy of being created. And you deserve to create them.

I want you — the *world* wants you — to feel openness and excitement about new experiences you're having and new discoveries you're making about yourself and about the world. The world wants you to create something new that exceeds your expectations and let go of old patterns and ways of life that don't serve you in your current life that you've grown out of.

I want to reassure you that just because you haven't made your move to France a reality yet, that doesn't mean that it won't happen or that it's not meant to be. Moving to a new country is a HUGE thing to do! You have to completely give up the life you have to create the life you want, and dedicate yourself to the pursuit of your dream, and that's really scary. There are no guarantees it will turn out like you want, or that you'll get the right job, or the right visa, that you'll meet the right partner, or even that that you'll be able to move here or be able to stay. An international relocation takes a lot of organizing, and has of moving pieces. You have to organize the end of your life as you know it, and conceive of a completely new life for yourself in France.

Big dreamers understand that there are three phases they must navigate in order to bring a dream from the imagination into reality. First, you must imagine it and know that what you want is possible generally. It is usually easy to prove to yourself that it's possible to move to France, as many have gone before you, and you may even be able to find evidence that others have moved to France and do whatever it is you want to do. Next, you must believe that it is possible for you, theoretically. And finally, you must believe that you deserve it and that it is within your reach, now.

My client Jasmine came to me after an immigration lawyer screwed up her case. She had been in France for several years, and was a photographer - a hugely talented photographer, at that.

She had been in France on several different visas, first as a student learning French, then on a Long Stay Visitor visa she'd gotten when she'd PACSed her French partner, to the vie privée after they'd been living together for more than a year, then back to Visitor after they'd broken up. Despite the failed relationship and her inability to work in France while a visitor, she loved living in Paris, and didn't want to go home permanently. While she traveled regularly back to the US to work as a photographer and earn money to fund her life in France, she dreamed of being able to do photography all over Europe and help people to create magical wedding experiences.

She knew she was good at what she does, that her photos are beautiful, and that she deserved to create a life for herself pursuing her dream.

There was only one problem: her visa status. An immigration lawyer had helped her to put together an application for a change of status in Paris, and then, when that failed, a new "profession liberale" visa application in the US, but both were turned down, for two reasons.

One: she was unsure of being able to make enough money for the "profession libérale autoentrepreneur" visa by doing just one type of photography, so she wrote a business plan including *every* type of photography she was capable of doing, from weddings and portraits to real estate listings to tourist photo shoots. Her business plan was unfocused and lacked detail, and a skeleton of what it should have been. (The lawyer, to whom she had paid an obscene sum of money, just collected the documents, but didn't help with actually putting together the business plan or tell her how to make her application stronger.) She didn't translate the detail of the dream in her head onto the page, which made it look like she didn't quite know what she was doing.

Two: To make matters worse, the wording on her website suggested that she was *already* working in Paris, on the Visitor visa, even though she technically didn't have the right to be working. She wasn't - she had just prepared her website as part of creating her business idea, but the préfecture and later, the consulate, didn't see it that way.

In the game of French bureaucracy, you only need one strike to be out, and that was two.

After multiple failures to change her status, the lawyer ended up having to get her a new "Visitor" visa status, and she lost all of that accumulated time she had spent in France as a student and then as the PACS partner of a French citizen, and she had to start ALL over on her immigration procedures and on her track to becoming a French permanent resident and citizen. She could have given up, or found it too frustrating and upsetting to have to continue spending time and money on regularizing her visa status. She could have decided, as many people do in this situation, to work in a non-so-legal way, which would have prevented her from paying taxes, from staying on French healthcare, and would have ultimately made it so much more difficult to fix her status later.

She didn't get upset, or frustrated. She held on tight too her belief in her photography business and her ability that things would work out in the end.

We began working together by renewing her existing visa and developing a plan for her change of status. I explained the problems with her previous application and asked her what she wanted to focus on - and we discussed strategies for ensuring the Préfecture wouldn't get the wrong idea.

I helped her to renew her visitor visa, so she could apply for a change of status directly in France, without going back to the US *again*, and then, we got to work on her business plan.

We niched down her business, focusing on her main skill sets and the type of photography she REALLY wanted to be doing. We got her letters of support from friends, previous clients, and a few potential clients who wanted to hire her for their ongoing photography needs. We set her rates and projected her finances.

It was a long, drawn out process, especially since the prefecture requested more information about her marketing strategies and business structure after we submitted her dossier, as DIRECCTE thought it looked like she was starting a photography studio - requiring more money and more equipment - and wanted to be sure that she could pay her business expenses. (She's actually an autoentrepreneur).

It took over a year before she FINALLY got her carte de séjour, but now, Jasmine is doing an AMAZING job, photographing events all over the city, and traveling to other parts of France. Last year, she had her photos featured in a national publication, and she continues to thrive as she has secured her 4-year carte de séjour, is engaged again to a French man, and is well on her way to permanent French residency and naturalization.

Big Dreamers decide to grow into their dream by planning holistically and for the long-term.

In my book _Foolproof French Visas_, I go through each of the different visa options for moving to France in detail, and identify different paths for beginning with a particular visa type and using various progressions to ultimately be able to apply for residency or naturalization. But before Big Dreamers identify exactly which visa type they'll apply for or which path suits them best, they understand the four main ways to move to France, and they begin with the vision they have for their ideal future.

What many Americans (and people of other nationalities, too) fail to understand is that being an immigrant in a country does not confer the same rights and privileges that you have in your home country, and that your plans are necessarily constrained by the confines and restrictions of your visa type. It is not as simple as applying for "a work visa," and then showing up and getting a job or figuring out how to earn money. You can't show up with a student visa and then get a full-time job, or come for a full-time job and then decide to quit to start your business. Each visa type has its own rules for what you are and are not allowed to do, and deviating from those rules can cause problems with the tax people and with renewing the visa and applying for residency.

That's why I invite my clients to dream big.

Sometimes, the people I speak with are looking for any way to get to France, and don't care how it happens. They want the quickest, easiest visa type, and don't care if it gives them the professional opportunities they want or even enables them to stay long-term. In some cases, they've already moved to France on a temporary visa type, or one that doesn't lead to residency or naturalization, and they come to me to figure out how to fix it, so they can do what they want to do. It is a lot harder to fix a less-than-ideal visa situation than it does to try to do things correctly in the first place. And a change of status can take a over a year, which means you'd spend lots of time in visa limbo while your dreams and plans stagnate.

A woman I did a consultation with, Joanne, who did not become a client, came to France on a visitor visa with plans to develop a business idea and then switch to the necessary status. Though we didn't work together, she kept me posted on her application's progress as she submitted the change-of-status request through her local préfecture in Strasbourg. After over 6 months with no response, they finally told her that it could take up to 2 years to process her application, and in the meantime, she wouldn't be able to open her business, finalize the purchase of the property she wanted to buy for her business location, or begin any kind of commercial activity. Ultimately, she decided to return to the US to apply for a new visa from scratch, and fortunately, her application was processed much more quickly. But the time and the opportunity cost of moving to France with the wrong visa type and attempting to switch were significant.

Instead of trying to find the fastest or easiest way to get to France, I work with my clients to develop a holistic future plan for their life so we can imagine the possibilities and the different visa scenarios for bringing their dreams to life.

If you want to make and sell art, it doesn't make any sense to apply for an au pair visa to get a foot in the door, or to do a license professionnelle in graphic design leading to an internship at a French company. If your goal is to work for a French company with a full-time contract, it doesn't make sense to apply for a visa to start your own business as a freelancer or autoentrepreneur. If your goal is a family visa allowing you to do any type of professional work or contract, it doesn't make sense to get PACSed instead of married, or to come as a tourist or a language student first.

Any long-term plan that is truly worth pursuing will almost always work out if we take the right approach, because being in France with the right visa types for over 5 years and gaining a visa type that is renewable indefinitely will almost inevitably enable you to apply for residency or naturalization successfully within 5-7 years. Once you have secured the coveted 10 year card or French passport, you will be able to do whatever you want. Legally and within reason, of course.

Planning for your life 5-10 years in the future considering all of your goals holistically, and taking the first concrete steps that lead towards those goals, can lessen the frustration and confusion you feel during the course of your first few years in France.

The process I use with my clients helps them to identify their unique skills and talents and some of their major life goals, so we can use that information to find the best stepping stones to the right French visa to start.

Envision your ideal professional life. What do you want it to look like in 3-5 years after you're successfully established in France? What are you doing for work or income, and how are you using your most important skills and talents to contribute positively to the world? What aspects of your professional life are most important to you?

Envision your personal growth: How have you grown personally and professionally? What obstacles have you overcome? What challenges have you faced that have helped you to grow as a person? How have you become stronger and more resilient? How have you created new adventures for yourself or had more fun?

Once you've dne the important work of dreaming and envisioning, you can begin the practical work of identifying the next steps or action items.

Fact-Finding: How do you get there? Employment? Starting a business or freelancing activity you can do from anywhere? Studying to employment? Are you financially able to retire? What visa type or types help you to pursue the professional development you want? What are ALLL the questions you have about moving that you have? Are there any deal-breakers or answers that affect your move date? Learn about the *9 Areas of Franceformation* and how to do the very practical day-to-day stuff, like figuring out which documents you need to bring with you, when and how to get them translated, how to transfer your driver's license, how to enroll your children in school, and approximately eleventy-billion practical admin tasks that will require the patience of a driver behind tractor-trailer participating in an Opération Escargot strike on the périphérique during rush hour.

Figure out the money: Get the job, start the business, save the money, whatever. Which one are you going to do? Are you qualified to do it in France? What does your industry / salary look like in France? Do you know how much it costs to move? How much will you save? How long will it take you to save it? Do you have blocks about getting money and saving money, which means that as soon as you get a significant sum of money set aside, you'll have a car problem, or another unexpected expense?

Set your moving date: Get your plane ticket and put together your visa application. What documents are you going to need? What's the timeline for the visa application once you have the job or employment figured out?

Arrange the rest of your life around your move: sell your belongings, give notice on your lease / sell your house, arrive in France and set up all the things. Do you know all the things you have to set up and do once you arrive? Imagine having to research each topic on your own and sorting through conflicting advice, and doing ALL of this simultaneously, while packing all of the emotional baggage of leaving behind your home and your current life as well.

Addressing these steps in order, without trying to do them all at the same time, will prevent you from becoming overwhelmed as you identify the best path for your move and navigate the challenges of making your Franceformation happen.

Today, I want to tell you about my client and friend Lola, who came to France in July 2017.

Lola wanted to come to France ever since she spent her spring semester studying abroad in Paris, and just knew she had to come back. In that way, she was a lot like me - I spent my whole second semester of my junior year in Paris planning how I would return as soon as possible. I even debated not leaving!

But Lola, who's Canadian, had lived in the US, and Singapore, and all over the world, and she was working in an art history museum in the US when she found me.

Now, the thing I love about her story is that Lola totally claims to have "manifested" me. Having seen the movie The Secret about attracting what you want into your life, Lola had taken steps towards manifesting her move to Paris LONG before she figured out how she was going to make it happen. She just didn't know how it was possible.

She had Paris-themed deco in her bathroom and a "Take me to Paris!" button on her winter coat. She KNEW with every fibre of her being that she was making the move, and she already had the important elements of her life in Paris imprinted in vivid detail in her mind. She knew what her skills were, what her passions were, and what she wanted to do in life: share her love of art and of Pairs with the world, while living in the city center.

She began researching. And she stumbled across my Facebook group, Americans in France.

We set up a call, and she told me about how she LOVED

her museum job, had majored in art history in college, and how her favourite part of studying in Paris was the Museum Studies class - where she had gotten to go to a different museum every class period, three times a week, and learn EVERYTHING about Paris art and history.

I asked her if she had ever thought about becoming a tour guide, and explained that she could get a "profession liberale" visa to work as a freelance tour guide for multiple companies in Paris, who are always enthusiastic about hiring autoentrepreneur tour guides with art history degrees. Her experience and her passion for art history and French history aligned perfectly with her museum experience, making her an ideal candidate for this type of job.

She'd have no trouble finding work with one or more of these companies, I explained, and she could even create her own tour experiences on platforms like AirBnb Experiences or her own website. The best part about this type of

And BOOM, just like that. Lola had her "how."

Over about 2 months, I helped Lola put together her

business plan for her profession liberal visa application, drawing on her museum experience, love of Paris and all things art history, and her university studies to create a fan-freaking-tastic visa application package.

Today, Lola is a thriving tour guide in Paris, living on l'Ile Saint-Louis and working for 3 tour companies, making BANK during tourist season, and traveling to all kinds of fantastic places - from champagne producers near Reims, to the Normandy beaches and Mont Saint Michel, to walking tours of Montmartre and the Eiffel Tower.

She recently renewed her initial visa and she is well on her way to French residency, and as long as she continues her success, she'll be able to live and work in France indefinitely.

Big Dreamers decide that there is no right time, so now is the right time.

With making any major change in your life, there is no easily definable or identifiable "right time." Many people who take the leap and move to France do have certain parameters for their move – they know a job is ending, or they're finishing school, or they know that they will have time to prepare for their new project and visa application at a certain time of the year when their job is slightly less busy. Other clients plan the move around their new projects, to ensure they get work easily upon arrival. A client who works in bookkeeping and tax preparation chose to focus on her application in the late spring and early summer, after tax season, while another client working as a tour guide wanted to arrive a couple of months before high tourist season officially started in Paris, so she could make connections and find work easily.

For some people, this can be practical. There is no sense in planning to move before finishing university or when a retirement pension is within reach. But I've also seen it often used as an excuse by those waiting for everything to fall into place, mostly surrounding their work, and it can be a way to sabotage the moving process. Applying for dozens of jobs before you understand the visa requirements and process or the French job market, for example, and deciding that the 'right time' will be when you find a job willing to sponsor you, is usually a way to ensure that the move is not going to happen, or if it does, that it will be a complete fluke. Envisioning what you want, understanding the requirements and How Things Work, and then continuing to work the plan while allowing everything to happen in its own time is a much more effective strategy in the long-term.

You may not ever feel like you're 100% ready, and there may always be valid reasons to push back your move or good, strategic reasons to wait. Ultimately, you'll be ready to make the move when you make the commitment and decide that it's happening, no matter what.

Recognize you won't ever completely rid yourself of doubt or fear.

It's easy to believe that the 'right time' to do something is when it doesn't feel scary anymore, and work to diminish the fear or doubt before you begin the moving process. As a sufferer of anxiety, I also used to try to lessen my fear or wait until the I felt more sure before I took action.

Do you know where that leads?

It leads to a lot of missed opportunities and disappointment, because by the time you're ready, the opportunity has moved on. It's not helpful to make decisions or take action from a place of fear, but it's equally unhelpful to expect fear or doubt to go away completely. Those feelings are part of being human and they're an integral part of doing something new and unlike anything you've ever done before. Moving to a completely new place with a visa process and a foreign language, potentially thousands of miles away from your family and friends, understandably inspires at least some nervousness.

In her book *Big Magic* about living a creative life, author Elizabeth Gilbert talks about how she sees fear as a part of life that is always along for the ride. In order to live creatively and pursue her dreams, she decided that in order to be successful, she would not try to fight fear; however, she regularly reminds fear that if it comes along with her for the journey, it is never allowed to drive, nor is it allowed to fiddle with the radio stations. Don't expect fear to get out of the car, and definitely don't expect to leave it at home when you move, but do put on your noise-blocking headphones and refuse to listen to any of its nonsense.

It would be weird if you weren't a little bit nervous.

But the secret to making the fear go away isn't waiting it out, it's action. It's taking action towards your dream in a productive, structured way, and understanding the process and how your next steps will lead you closer to your goal.

Understand The Law of Diminishing Intent

I watch all the time as people with the best of intentions push back their move again and again, waiting for "enough" money or the right job to magically come to them, only to find out several years down the line that they've taken a new job in their home country and have decided to reconsider moving to France when they find the right job or they're retired.

It reminds me of those couples who got engaged and say they'll get married "in 2 to 3 years." You congratulate them, and then you see them again a few months later, and the timeline hasn't changed. It hasn't become "we'll get married in 1.5-2.5 years." It's still 2-3 years. Usually, these couples end up being engaged for 5-6 years and some never even make it down the aisle. Other couples get engaged, immediately discuss approximately when they'd like to get married - enough time to invite out-of-town guests, schedule a spring or fall wedding, determine the size of the party, the budget, and the venue - and commit to these small decisions rather quickly, so they have a timeline for taking the most important actions.

At some point, if you don't actually start making movement and planning your goal, it's just a dream that risks being unfulfilled, and the only way to turn a dream into an achievable goal is through planning, taking action, and setting a deadline. It's just a nice daydream about wouldn't it be nice if it were "something you could do someday."

The problem with plans for "someday" is that they never seem to get done, because we never begin taking action on them. It's called the Law of Diminishing Intent: the longer you wait to do something, the less likely you are to ever actually do it.

It is often said that the best time to plant a tree was 20 years ago, and the second-best time is now. Similarly, the best time to take action on anything is now, while you are eager and excited about it, and before you get bogged down in the details of what, when, and how.

Commit to the next logical step, without creating unnecessary detours.

Sometimes my clients (or potential clients I talk to) want to "try it out" for a few weeks, or months, or a year with a temporary visa or a longer vacation living like a local, and I always encourage them to question their reasons for doing so. In many cases, they want time on the ground in France to work out the details before they jump through the hoops of applying for one of the long-stay visa types. In other words, they don't trust that they can work out the details along with the visa application.

I always tell them the same thing: there are lots of good reasons to apply for the visa immediately instead of waiting (the law of diminishing intent being a good one), and you can always come back if things don't work out and you don't want to finish out your year. Conversely, there are many reasons why a "pre-trip" to "get settled" in France or scope things out without the visa is a bad one.

First of all, you can never apply for a visa directly in

France, so you absolutely have to return to your home country within 90 days to do your visa application. Every few weeks, I see a post on social media about someone who "moved to France" without thinking it through - also known as, they got on a plane - and are now wondering how to apply to stay. They can't. The trip becomes an added expense and a delay, when the money could have been better spent on visa application assistance or been used sitting in the bank to support the visa application. A vacation to France, however well-intended, is not a move.

Secondly, most French bureaucratic procedures, from opening a bank account to signing up for any useful service, require proof of address and therefore a long-term lease. All of those things are quite difficult to get without a long-term visa. Some of them, like a long-term lease, are difficult even *with* the visa, and not having proof of staying long-term is going to complicate the apartment rental applications. Someone who arrives without a visa in hand should not expect to get much useful stuff done that would make them feel like their move was progressing, and would actually feel counter-productive.

Thirdly, if you are looking for work, being on the ground in France without a visa is going to be more discouraging than anything else. It will be quite difficult to get anyone - client or company - to commit to hiring you without a visa, and it can make the visa process seem all that more daunting when it appears as though you are striking out with your employment search on the ground. Instead, approaching potential clients or employers with a clear visa plan and a timeline for when you will arrive in France will be far more effective for finding work opportunities, and people will be far more receptive to you in just about any situation (hiring you or assisting you with administration) when you are not merely a tourist.

Finally, applying for a visitor visa with the intention of looking for work, or of staying with a partner you are not married to, are both red flags to the French consulate, which will likely reject your application. I discuss this further in _Foolproof French Visas_, but generally, changing visa statuses (or planning too change) soon after your arrival in France is not possible, and having a rejected visa application to overcome can make subsequent visa applications all the more difficult.

If you want to live in France for an extended period of time, whether that is a year or more or whether you'd like to try too stay indefinitely, the best course of action is to plan as though you'll be staying forever, applying for French residency and/or naturalization when the time comes, and planning your visa progression to ensure staying will be possible. You can always decide at a moment's notice to pick up and move back home if things aren't working out, but fixing or recalibrating a misguided visa application or a temporary or nonrenewable visa type into something that enables you to extend your stay is far more complex and not always possible. Committing to the next logical step in a well-thought-out and sustainable plan rather than leaping ahead and trying to do everything at once will help to make your move more successful.

Deciding doesn't mean forcing or being reckless.

Making a decision and taking action on your move to France before you are ready doesn't mean being reckless or throwing caution to the wind so you can get on a plan next week. It's not about forcing yourself to be ready before you are; instead, it means that you begin taking action, however small, towards your move. Sometimes, the big, dramatic gestures are empty, but regular and consistent actions towards your dream will add up quickly.

Deciding means that instead of just reading blogs about

being lost in cheeseland or fretting on social media posts about how to do your taxes and avoid international taxation and exchange your driver's license (tasks that will take care of themselves AFTER you have arrived!), you actually begin taking steps to get your life in order so that the move becomes more realistic as time goes on. Of course it's important to dream and to fuel your desire to move to France, and it's important to visualize what you want your life to look like after you arrive. But, it's equally important to have a realistic view of where you are now versus where you want to be, and can identify the next right thing (or A next right thing) to do in each area of your life to get ready.

Deciding is showing up regularly to move forward, whether it's putting a little money aside each month or each paycheck to your France savings account, and finding some way to get started now, even when the material reality of your move could be far off.

Many of my clients are people who *want* to be ready to move to France before they speak with me for the first time, and they become ready during our Clarity Call and as they commit to working together on their visa application. Other people have been following me and my business for

years on social media or by email before they make the
decision to move, because they want to work out all of the
finer details of their relocation before they take the first
step. While sometimes, the caution makes sense, it's also
caused problems when a plan they're working towards
becomes more difficult or impossible to execute due to rule
changes or even changes in their family circumstances. I
don't ever encourage my clients to recklessly leave
everything behind if they aren't ready and don't have the
financial support in place to be able to make the move a
success, but I also don't sugarcoat the possibility that the
longer they wait, the more motivation they lose and the
more likely there are to get stuck in their current situation.

Amanda first contacted me by email around 2014, and had
apparently been following my work through my former
website, Paris Unraveled, for more than a year at that
point. She was Australian, but had traveled to France
several times and dreamed of finding a way to immigrate
permanently. Her level of French was low-intermediate,
but we decided that the best way for her to come to France
and transition into being able to live and work here in the
long-term was to study French before enrolling in a degree
program in a French university, which would allow her to
apply for a job. She was in her late 30s, which meant she

had aged out of programs like Work Holiday or Au Pair which would have enabled her to come to France more easily. A student visa for a full-time language program would enable her to have a part-time job on the side, we reasoned, which would help her to fund her studies.

I spoke to her several times over the course of 2-3 years, but each time, she had a reason why she wasn't ready or couldn't make the commitment. She wanted to improve her French. She wanted to save money, but never seemed to be able to. Finances were her biggest barrier to being able to make the transition, but finally (maybe a relative gave her a gift?), she was able to begin the visa application and make the move, around summer of 2017. The only problem was that French consulates in Australia (and in many countries) were no longer issuing long-stay renewable student visas for language studies that would enable her to get a part-time job. They had begun, with little warning, issuing only "temporary stay" visas for language studies, which foiled her plan to support herself and ultimately renew her visa to pursue a master's. If she had applied for her visa even 6 months earlier, she would have been able to embark on the dream we had outlined together. Instead, waiting for the "right time" and for everything to be in order meant that the "right time" never came. Unwilling (or unable) to find another solution and to invest more time and energy in developing another plan, Amanda unfortunately wasn't able to move to France.

Another person who consulted with me briefly, Michael, ended up in a similar predicament when the enforcement of rules surrounding autoentrepreneur registration suddenly became stricter. When we first met, I explained to him as I did with all of my clients, that students were not eligible for autoentrepreneur status, and were only allowed to work 20 hours per week as employees, not self-employed. At the time, several years ago, the official legal guidance wasn't clear, and many students around the internet bragged about how they were able to register their autoentrepreneur activity with no problems, and were rarely caught by the préfecture or the tax office as having done something inappropriate. The autoentrepreneur website to register a new activity allowed anyone to register, and seemingly didn't care when students or even visitors sent in a copy of their visa which disallowed work or self-employment.

I gave Michael the option of doing things "the right way" and applying for the profession libérale - entrepreneur visa type, which would put his business activity no the up-and-up, but the process was more arduous and expensive than he wanted to undertake. Besides, he convinced himself that I was wrong, since "so many people" had had success doing exactly that thing. He was convinced that they didn't care. So instead, he came to France with a student visa, enrolled in a language class, with plans to develop his business as a student and then switch his status after his program ended. He hoped to stay under the radar until he was successful.

You can probably guess what happened next. Although he had been fully warned that he may not be successful with his autoentrepreneur registration, he was nonetheless surprised when his registration was returned to him, with a letter telling him that due to his student visa status, he was unable to register as an autoentrepreneur and his application could not be processed. According to people telling their stories online, this same thing had worked for so many people doing things "the wrong way," and he got caught out. Suddenly, he was in France on a valid student visa but unable to pursue the opportunity he wanted, and he couldn't switch statuses in France or register his activity easily. His new choices were to try to find some other part-time job to support himself while in France, or to return to the US to start over with the correct visa type. Failing to heed professional advice while taking shortcuts to the visa process recommended by strangers online created a difficult situation that could have been avoided.

Big Dreamers decide to seek help along the way.

If you've followed me so far, I have no doubts about your ability to make things happen, to bring your dreams to life, and to make your *Franceformation* a reality. But what I do know, from being a big dreamer myself, is that my dreams come true far more quickly and easily when I have help and guidance along the way.

The thing about big dreamers like you is that you're highly motivated, highly competent, and probably used to doing things on your own. I commend you for that, because you're the one who has your best interests at heart and who knows what you truly want in life. The challenge can come when you believe that because you are *capable* of doing it yourself, that you *have to* do it yourself. You end up frustrated and discouraged, and things take longer than you expect, because you don't have support and you don't know where you're going.

What if I told you it was okay to have help and guidance along the way, or even have someone do most of the work for you? What if I told you that having assistance from someone who knows you, who understands what you want to create, and who knows the *Franceformation* process, would help you to create something more easily than you can imagine, remove the frustration, and make the process fun and enjoyable?

When you focus on what they CAN do, outsource what you *don't have to* do, and on choose to enjoy the process, it can go a lot faster than you expect and create better results.

Know where not to expect help.

I've got a bit of bad news for you. In the English-speaking world, we have the idea that someone who works for the government is a "public servant." That person's job is to help you, and in many cases, they do. They try to inform, to find you the answers you need, and to generally provide service to the public.

There's no such thing as a "public servant" in France. Instead, government employees are called "fonctionnaires." They fulfil a function. They are, quite literally, cogs in a machine. And their job is not to serve, but to determine whether the question or task you bring them is part of their official function. If it is, and all of the elements are provided so they can do their job, they fulfil the function. If not - if they don't know what to do, or if an important element is missing - the task cannot be completed. You get bounced to someone new and put off for another day, which can be frustrating, especially when it happens multiple times, with multiple people, and you can't get help or a straight answer.

The problem with this structure, then, is that officially, there is no "public service" element to any department's work. Nobody at the préfecture is tasked with knowing how visa types interact with French tax law or social charge collections. There isn't even a specific employee tasked with answering questions by phone or email, so your queries go unanswered. And if you do get someone willing to help, they may not always be able, because they are not trained on the broader workings of the immigration system and have no interest in learning, as it's not part of their job.

Assistance and feedback from government officials tends to be myopic and focused only on that person's department and the immediate question at hand, when what you need is assistance that anticipates your needs and considers the bigger picture of the life you want to create.

All help is not created equal.

There is a LOT of information on the internet about moving to France and on any topic you can imagine related to immigration. But it's not all equally valuable. It's not all good. I have seen lots of people flounder or misstep during the immigration process because they outsource every question they have to a different Facebook group, where the people replying have varying experiences and have all gone through the process a different number of years ago. And none of them have any experience with visas and immigration beyond their own individual experience, some of which is extremely outdated.

It reminds me of a cartoon I've seen floating around the internet, possibly with Snoopy and Peppermint Patty. Advice: $0. Good advice: $2.

Back in the quaint olden days, before the internet, we used to naively believe that access to information was a big problem, and that things would be different if only more people just knew more stuff or could learn more easily. As it turns out, that wasn't actually the problem. We now have more information than ever before, and more information is created each day than was created in the entire history of humanity pre-2000. Or something. But now, we also have to carefully sort through the information, and consider its source, and determine which aspects apply to our situation. It can be exhausting, and it's rarely worth your time and effort.

Having someone on your team who has already done the work for you of distinguishing fact from fiction and who can more easily parse what it's important for you to know in your specific situation can be priceless.

Outsourcing enables you to focus on your Zone of Genius.

Even for my clients who are well-established professionals in their field and NOT starting a new business from scratch, the topic that causes the most stress is their ability to find clients and make professional connections in France once they arrive. It can be extremely difficult to search for jobs or find potential clients when you don't yet have the ability to work in France, and the professional connections you make can be reluctant to count on you or to plan for future projects until your visa is in your hand. Having relocation assistance and clarity on your future visa situation and timeline can enable you to communicate more assuredly about your impending arrival in France, and allow you to focus on your skillset and your zone of genius, so you can spend your time on professional development and making connections that will help further your career once in France.

Getting help allows you to focus your energy and avoid doubt.

When you are focused on a large and complex project like moving to France, it's easy to get distracted by all of the moving pieces, and it can be difficult to see the big picture and *how* you will move through the *Franceformation* process. If you have never moved to France before, it can be impossible to see the big picture and to understand the next right actions to take to effectively move your relocation forward. Doing the wrong things, or spending too much time on inconsequential details, can be frustrating and time-wasting, and can cause you to doubt your plans and to waste valuable energy that could be moving your relocation forward.

You deserve to have help along the way. You deserve to have someone there with you, to explain how to proceed, to identify your options, to talk you through the consequences and the implications of each decision, from your visa choice to your choice of cell phone service company. You deserve to have an ally during your

Franceformation, who can help you to anticipate the challenges to come, to give you the tools you need, and to be your advocate in the face of French administration and culture shock alike.

This is your new life we're talking about. And if you're ready to change it for the better, and committed to your *Franceformation*, I'm here for you.

Monica was an immensely talented luxury interior designer who began working with me as the temporary work contract (CDD) that had enabled her to get a European Blue Card drew to a close. While she loved her work and was eager to continue working with the same company that had employed her, they had a very small number of salaried employees and worked primarily with contractors. They wanted to keep her on and continue dazzling their own clients with Monica's talents, but the firm managers were inflexible in their policies regarding hiring long-term employees on CDIs (indefinite work contracts in France). So she'd have to find another way to remain in France.

When we began working together, she already had all of the elements she needed to put together an excellent application for the "Compétences et Talents" visa, a visa type for experienced professionals with high incomes which was discontinued in 2016. She had an international professional network ready and willing to hire her on a project-basis, an impressive portfolio, and a plan to create a great income for her new business. The only thing she didn't have was the time or the energy to compile her own visa application on top of her demanding full-time work.

When someone with Monica's credentials and background prepares to move to France, or, as in her case, ask for a new visa status while here, her experience and capabilities tend to speak for themselves, and the process of putting together the visa application is simple and exciting. It becomes a matter not of creating a business or identifying a client base, but of showcasing her unique talents and skills in a way that highlights her future contributions to her industry in France. For Monica, hiring someone else to create the visa application is a matter of being able to spend time focusing her creative energy on her own work, rather than spending time on an important project outside of her zone of genius. Of course a highly creative and competent professional can easily put together an application that will pass muster with the authorities, but writing the application wasn't the best use of Monica's time, and it may not be the best use of yours.

Monica had the vision of what she wanted to do, the talent to back it up, and the main thing she wanted was someone to just take care of everything for her while she continued to focus on her work. She painted the broad strokes of where her project was going and the type of work she'd like to continue doing long into the future, in Europe, the United States, and around the world, while I took care of the details and of putting together all of the aspects of her plans into a viable presentation for the préfecture.

The biggest challenge to her application came when the visa rules changed one month after her visa application for "Compétences et Talents" was submitted. That visa type ceased to exist, and though her application had been submitted before the deadline, they wanted additional documentation so they could change her status instead to one of the new "Passeport Talent" visa types. Without assistance, Monica would have had to research and ask questions about the new visa types herself, in French, to préfecture officials who themselves had only a vague understanding of how the new visa types would work. It would have taken time away from her job to negotiate a new understanding of the visa types and to figure out which one to apply for. Instead, she had assistance throughout the process and was able to continue focusing on her future design agency while I revised her application and informed her of what we'd have to put together to meet the new visa guidelines.

Today, Monica runs a successful design firm in Paris and works with clients and major design firms internationally, and is creating an online learning platform for art, architecture, and design students to work in English and French.

When Big Dreamers find the way, they blossom into a fuller, more authentic version of themselves.

As humans, if we are not growing, expanding, and learning new things, then we are shrinking and stagnating, causing us to feel negative emotions, lose confidence in ourselves, have low self-esteem, and give up on our goals and dreams. Conversely, by leaning into the discomfort and challenges of a new adventure in France, we are called to figure out how to navigate the endless bureaucracy and master a whole new set of tools.

Adapting to a new cultural environment means developing a new set of skills: intellectual skills, like language development, personal development skills, such as resilience and empathy, and cultural skills, like code-switching. Moving to a new country forces you to evaluate and refocus every single part of your life, from your personal possessions and what's important to you, to maintaining significant relationships, to finding ways to develop personally and professionally in an unfamiliar work environment, to creating new habits and a new lifestyle. During the process of your Franceformation, you'll have to take complete stock of your life, decide what goes and what stays, negotiate keeping the things you want to keep (emotionally, spiritually, and physically), and pack up all of your physical and metaphorical baggage.

No matter how old you are or how emotionally and spiritually grounded you are, an international move is a catalyst for unprecedented personal growth.

And in confronting and overcoming the many challenges along the way, you will reveal who you really are, what you are truly capable of, and gain in confidence, independence, and resilience. You will be someone you've never been before, and you will do things you've never done before. You will evolve. You will blossom. And you will become. At each stage of the process, you can choose to shrink, or you can choose to grow.

If you choose to grow, the skills, qualities, and intelligences you develop will serve you in every area of your life, from your career to your interpersonal relationships. And if your personal growth has stagnated for a while because you've been in the same career or relationship, you will exercise long-forgotten skills, like developing your ability to imagine something big that you *really* want, beyond the natural or logical next step in your existing life. You will reignite your imagination and stoke your desire for newness and adventure, and put skills like emotional intelligence and empathy to use in new ways.

You may expand or pivot your career. Many times, people get caught up in trying not to change too much about their new life in France, when the job they have doesn't exactly exist in the same way it exists in their home country. When the salaries aren't comparable, or the opportunities don't seem as interesting, you may fret, and worry that your plans for moving to France can't be realized. But, during the process of taking stock of your life and your dreams, you may realize that the move instead gives you the opportunity to expand, to take a leap of faith, and to pivot their education and experience into something related, but completely new and exciting. Instead of trying to recreate your current life in a new place by finding a similar job, you can take advantage of an exciting opportunity to focus on your true areas of genius and passion projects, to figure out what you truly want to pursue in life and how you can share your unique gifts with the world.

We don't have many opportunities in life to imagine the infinite possibilities of starting completely over in a positive way, and the "clean slate" you get when you begin a new adventure such as this one is truly unique. You get to begin anew with everything from your daily schedule and your job, to your habits, to your hobbies and activities. You get to decide who you will be and how you will confront new challenges. You get to grow as a human.

You will develop resilience, and learn, beyond what you have already experienced, to recover quickly from difficulties and experience tenacity and toughness. The person you become as you take on a new adventure and navigate your way through a labyrinthian bureaucratic system, while maintaining a firm belief in your dreams and in your future, will help you to exercise faith.

You will continue to develop new intellectual and emotional skills, from language skills, to cultural understanding and empathy, to your openness to new people and ideas, and to your growth as a human being. You will develop your language and communication skills, and become a better citizen of the world.

You get the experience of a lifetime, and potentially get the opportunity to become a French citizen, granting you access to the whole EU. You give your children the possibility of becoming bilingual, and open job markets and different educational options up to them. Freedom for you and for them to travel and pursue opportunities more freely. When you open yourself up to being anywhere opportunity leads you, you can live a more liberated life and be more authentically you.

When Big Dreamers doubt themselves, they lose faith in their dreams and in themselves.

I also speak with many people about their dream to move to France who never seem to get their act together and who always seem to be waiting for the next right thing to fall into place before they can begin the process. I am empathetic, of course, when someone who desperately wants to move can't seem to see the path that can open up before them, and in many cases, even if we discuss the opportunities they could have in France (a type of job or business or professional path), they demand 'proof' that it will work out and that they'll succeed before moving forward. In the absence of such proof, of the ability to see the top of the staircase, they find every excuse not to take the smallest first step.

Messages from people in this category pop up in my inbox regularly to tell me about their new deadline and lament that they should already be in France, living their dream. In the beginning of my career, I would get excited with them each time, telling them to go for it, that I believed in them, and that they were ready. But as much as I may believe in someone's ability to bring their dream to life, my words are worthless if they don't believe it themselves.

I used to think they meant, "I'm ready to get started now and to begin creating the life I've imagined."

What they really mean is that they are seeking validation, and setting themselves an arbitrary deadline for "being ready" and are hoping to force themselves into feeling more ready by the new time they've declared they want to start. Usually, not much has changed. And when it comes to beginning the process, they still want the answers before they are willing to invest the time and the effort into beginning the project.

When I tell them, "You can do it! Let's get started," these people retreat, satisfied that I believe in them and that their dream is still alive. Knowledge that someone believes in them is enough to satisfy them, but not enough to inspire them towards action.

And then, they realize that they have done this before, and they weren't really ready then, and they begin to doubt whether they are ready now. They have lost faith in themselves. Their level of belief doesn't match my level of belief in them. The process begins again, and each time, they are a little less sure they can make it work out. Sometimes, they begin the process again, redoing things they have already tried: applying to jobs that can't sponsor them, learning French with free apps in hopes of one day (several years down the line) enrolling in a French degree program while working, or getting a temporary visa to work as an au pair or to study French, without a clear path for getting out of the temporary situation and creating a stable and secure

Not following through with your decision to move to France doesn't only mean that you don't end up living in France. Sacrificing a dream because you believe you can't make it come true has repercussions on your self-esteem, your belief in yourself, and your general ability to believe that you can do the things you say you want to do. Giving up on one dream, and deciding you are not worthy of it, forces you to dream smaller, to think incrementally, and to impose limits on what you believe you are capable of. Not taking that one leap of faith makes you question, in the future, whether you can take others, until you are reduced to living your life in baby steps.

And if you are consistently working on just the next thing you believe you can do, without a larger plan or goal in mind that you can believe in, you are setting yourself up for a life of unfulfilled promises to yourself.

The question you have to ask yourself is not, "will this work out for me?"

For virtually everyone I speak with, we are able to work out a way for them to move to France, and find a path forward for them that feels exciting, yet doable. Almost every dream can turn into a plan, and the only thing it costs is your willingness to examine it. Knowing something is possible for you, and turning it down, is different from believing something would never work out anyway.

The question is how much time you will spend waiting for the right time, and waiting for the pieces to fall into place, before you commit to living your dream. And the question is how you will feel about your dream, and about yourself, in 5 years, or 10 years, if you are still waiting for things to work out instead of making them happen.

Life doesn't suddenly stop coming at you at breakneck speed to signal that it's time for you to do what you've always wanted to do. There will never be a rainbow that shines down upon you, and angels singing, and a literal sign that appears to tell you when it's time to go.

So, what will happen if you continue on the path you're currently on? The job you have might turn into a mortgage and a marriage and a couple of kids, making the move all that more difficult to imagine. Your current job might turn into a career you don't want to leave, or opportunities you don't want to miss out on, or the fear that your career in France may not match up to expectations you've set based on your career at home. None of those things are bad unless they make you feel trapped, and make it harder for you to live out your dreams.

If your life stays relatively the same over the next ten years, and you do what is expected of you, where does that path lead, and how will you feel while pursuing it? What regrets, if any, do you have?

And do you value yourself and your dreams enough to take a chance on pursuing them?

Big Dreamers like you can leverage expertise to enhance and accelerate your Franceformation journey.

Consider that your future dream life in France is a huge canvas, and right now, it is blank. Our job together is first to outline the image you want to paint, and then, to paint by number, filling in colors all over the canvas until the beautiful image emerges. At the moment, if you're not even sure what visa type you'll apply for, you may not be able to envision the future image at all. And yet, it's there. The life that you want to create for yourself is inside of you, and our most important task is to extract it, in all of its glory, without damaging it or telling you that for some reason, you can't have it.

Once we have played midwives to your new life goals, our next step is to nurture and protect them as they mature, and as we begin to paint inside the lines and bring the colors to life. In this stage, during the process of determining how to bring your dream to life, it's important to continually nourish it with positive energy and excitement, and to avoid naysayers and "realists" who will be "concerned" that you are wasting your time on something that may not come to fruition. You may have your own doubts during this stage, and it's important to question your doubts and fears to prevent them from taking over. Il faut cultiver son jardin — and pull the weeds as we go.

The higher your enthusiasm, your energy, and your belief in yourself, your project, and your ability to make the move, the faster we will be able to fill in the grid and bring your dream to live. We can quickly build momentum and create the outlines of your new life, but at the same time, we have to avoid moving too fast and burning out. It's a delicate balance, to build energy and momentum on one hand, while pacing ourselves on the other. If we're not careful, moving too fast, or *danser plus vite que la musique*, the first obstacle or challenge will derail your project and your belief in your ability to make it happen.

My unique Franceformation process is a holistic process to help you identify what you want to create in each area of your life, to guide you through the visa process for creating it, and to facilitate your passage through the administrative challenges that await you during the visa application procedure and upon arrival in France.

Before beginning, I recommend reading my book *Foolproof French Visas*, which enables you to identify your path to France and what type or types of visas you may want to apply for.

Once you have an idea of which type of immigration you'll pursue and what your goals are, we can schedule our initial free Franceformation Clarity Call, where we'll solidify your visa plans and your timeline, and set a tentative start date for our work together, along with a tentative visa application date, so we know when to make your visa appointment.

We'll discuss your overall readiness to make your move happen. A sense of "readiness" to take a big step isn't something that comes from outside of you. It is something that you create inside of you, and you do it by taking action. While sometimes my clients have concrete time constraints, like waiting for a child to graduate, or selling their house, many times, the time constraints are in their minds. During our call, we'll discuss what actual barriers there are to beginning your move process, and what barriers you've created in your mind to hold up the process.

As we begin our work together, you'll get access to my complete library of materials to prepare you for your move to France and the administrative work that awaits you upon arrival. From a moving checklist of documents to gather and things to do before you submit your visa application, to tutorials on post-arrival procedures like enrolling your kids in school, registering your business, or filing your first French tax return, you'll be accompanied along every step of your journey.

The 5 Foundations of the Franceformation system:

Throughout my years assisting people in moving to France, not only have I developed the expertise required to help them determine the right visa type for their goals and to achieve success, I've also developed a thorough understanding of the other tools and support you'll need as you move through the relocation process. Using my previous experience with many clients, I've developed useful documentation in five key areas to help you to fill in the colors of your Franceformation canvas more quickly and more vividly than you could do it on your own.

Mindset – When preparing for such a huge life changing event like an international move, your mindset is key, and questioning or reflecting on any doubts or challenges about your ability to move to France or your ability to bring your new dream life to fruition is key to ensuring your success. Cultivating your success mindset so you continue to grow personally and professionally is a lifelong journey, and I've put together a journal of questions for you to reflect on or answer for yourself to help you better develop

Money – Figuring out and preparing for financial security throughout the move is an important part of allowing you to feel secure during the process and confident in your ability to make the move work. It's also an important aspect of the visa application, in that a certain amount of money in cash is required for each type of visa. I've created a workbook and resources for you to calculate your expected expenses during the move, money coming in and out, and how to generate extra money to put towards your moving expenses and savings, to help you create a full-color picture of your finances as you develop your moving timeline.

Professional Development — Your career may look different in France, depending on your skills, professional experience, and ability to continue working in your same field, or not. Salaries in France are lower, benefits are higher, and overall, the ability to get a sponsored work visa can vary greatly based on your experience and salary expectations. While we will determine your likely visa path before even beginning the process, you'll have access to professional development workbooks and professional guidance on developing your career options or business ideas into full-fledged projects and plans. Once you have an idea of where your skills and experience could take you in France, we'll be able to put together a coherent and compelling strategy for your professional launch and future success in France.

Language – Speaking French, or being dedicated to learning, is essential to creating a successful and fulfilling life in France. While you'll need to find other tools and resources to improve your skills, I provide vocabulary lists for our most important bureaucratic endeavors and help you to identify the gaps in your language knowledge that you'll want to address quickly.

French Admin Preparation – There are lots of small admin tasks you can do to get ready for your move to France, from collecting copies of official documents like your birth certificate and driving record, to getting insurance documents necessary for the visa application. The admin and bureaucracy tasks you need to complete before your departure are broken down into bite-sized items you can do at your own pace, with an explanation of why you need to do each task and what you'll need each document for. Once you arrive, you'll receive access to a whole new set of informative videos, the *First 100 Days in France*, to walk you through each administrative step you need to do upon arrival to set up your life. Of course, depending on your service package, some packages include all of the French administration done for you during the first 100 days, with follow-up support available.

Decluttering the life you have now and letting go of various aspects of it is key to finding peace and happiness as part of your move. It's all too easy to bring the clutter (physical and emotional) with us, then wonder why we are frustrated, stagnant, and stuck in the new place as well as the old. Usually, when clients come to me to begin their Franceformation, they have already begun the process of ungrounding and of laying the groundwork for their new life in France.

Big Dreamers ask the right questions to align with their dream.

Determining when to make the move and figuring out how you know you're ready is one of the trickiest parts of embarking on your *Franceformation.* There are so many factors to consider when deciding the best way to approach creating something new, and it's easy to let practical considerations and the fear that you don't know *how* to do something to get in the way.

But, if you knew you were fully supported, and that things would work out for you no matter what you decide and no matter when you begin, what would you choose? Leaving aside the questions of how much money you need, or what kind of job you'll get (because we can figure out those things later), what do you actually want?

Before you determine what your next step is, I'd like you to consider each of the following seven questions. To answer them, I would advise you to go to a quiet spot where you'll be alone, and to write down your answers on an actual piece of paper. Don't just think through the topics, and don't discuss them with anyone, not even someone who would be relocating with you. Asking someone for advice or their opinion on your move is going to prevent you from listening to what you really want and from feeling your own feelings on the subject. Before you have taken significant action towards your goal, it's too early to involve other people and their opinions on your life.

So, get a journal or a blank piece of paper, and set a timer for 3-5 minutes for each question. Write what comes to mind. Don't censor yourself or worry about what anyone else will think. Just listen to your own thoughts and intuition on your Franceformation and let yourself identify how you truly feel.

Then, you can evaluate your readiness and determine what the next step is for you.

No matter where you are in your journey, it's okay. It's important not to force yourself to feel more ready than you are, or to judge what your feelings are about your move. Just be honest. You have plenty of time.

1. What is your current situation in life, and what factors are contributing to your desire to move? What do you want to leave behind, and what do you want to create or move towards?

2. What's not working for you right now as you prepare to move to France?

3. What have you already tried, and what hasn't worked?

4. What do you see as your 3 biggest obstacles to moving to France, or to making the decision to move too France?

5. If you don't make the move, what does your life look like in 5 years? In 10 years? How do you feel? Are you happy with the way your life turned out?

6. If you DO make the move to France, imagine it's 10 years in the future. What does your life look like? What have you created for yourself? How do you feel? Are you satisfied with your decisions?

7. What do you need to feel secure that moving to France is the right decision for you right now?

A friend and mentor of mine likes to say, "Fear is excitement without the breath." So, take a deep breath in. Count to 4 as you breathe in, hold it for 4, and breath out for 4. Do this 4 times.

Now, close your eyes, and ask yourself the following questions.

Imagine that you begin your Franceformation now. How does that feel in your body?

Next, imagine that you decide that you are not ready yet, and that you will begin in six months, in one year, or three years, or five years. How does each of those options feel?

Which option feels the lightest and the most exciting for you?

And, on a scale of 1 to 10, with 1 being not at all ready, and 10 being "I'm ready to move yesterday!", how would you rate your enthusiasm for moving to France and for getting started on your *Franceformation*?

Now you know when you'll be ready to get started.

If you feel ready to start now or think you'll be ready within 6 months:

If you're eager to get started and think you may be ready to move within the next few months, please don't hesitate to take the following steps so we can begin your Franceformation process:

1. Read Foolproof French Visas.

Even if you've done some prior research and have an idea of what visa type(s) you'll be eligible for, I highly recommend reading my book so you have a thorough understanding of the visa application process, the types of documents you'll need to provide, the required financial resources, and what we'll need to do to put together a successful application. Armed with a good understanding of your options, we'll be able to have a better, more in-depth discussion of your future in France and your relocation timeline during our call.

You can purchase *Foolproof French Visas* here: https://payhip.com/b/KG0z.

2. Join the Americans in France Facebook group.

I run a free Facebook group with nearly 11,000 members where we regularly discuss life in France, answer questions about French administration and bureaucracy, and assist those who are planning to move. I also regularly post tips and tricks for moving, answer questions about visas, and post offers for my books or to schedule calls with me. You do not have to be American to join, but please answer the questions so your profile will be accepted. I work hard to keep out spam and fake profiles so our group can be as active and as relevent as possible.

You can join it here:

https://www.facebook.com/groups/americansinfrance/

(There are many groups for Americans in France, in Paris, in Europe, and all kinds of things. Be sure to join the right group, as some of the groups are less than helpful!)

3. Schedule a free 45-minute Franceformation Clarity Call with me.

If you're planning to move, or at least begin the relocation process, within the next 6 months or so, please apply to schedule a free Franceformation Clarity Call with me. During the 45-minute call, we'll discuss your overall readiness, what you need to help you get ready to move forward, and we'll get to know each other to see if we're a good fit to work together on your *Franceformation.* Ideally, you'll leave the call clear on your next steps, know which *Franceformation* package is a good fit for your needs, and have a start date in mind for beginning work on your visa application.

Apply for a Franceformation Clarity Call here: www.yourfranceformation.com/clarity-call/

If you don't feel ready now or within 6 months:

If the option to begin creating your dream life and embark on your *Franceformation* now, or within 6 months, didn't feel like the lightest option for you, that's okay. There is no pressure to get started. If moving to France is meant to be for you, you have time. The opportunity will arise again when the time is right, and what you truly want in life will not pass you by. Do not pressure yourself to be ready if you aren't.

But not being ready NOW doesn't mean that you can't take action. In that case, I would encourage you to continue to get ready to get ready.

1. Create a plan to address the three main obstacles you feel are preventing you from being ready for your move.

What is the first step you can take towards addressing those obstacles? If the obstacles are financial or related to employment, how can you take steps towards financial security or develop skills that will be more easily transferrable to whatever you could plan to do in France?

2. Keep inspiring yourself to begin your Franceformation, and build momentum towards getting ready.

Do things that remind you of your excitement and enthusiasm for moving to France, whether that's reading novels or memoirs set in Paris, creating a vision board of the places you'll visit (or pastries you'll eat) when you arrive, and continue working on learning French. Having faith that you will be ready soon and that you are continually moving towards your goal will motivate you

3. Schedule in time to reread this book and revisit the questions.

Almost all adults have known a couple who gets engaged, saying they want to get married in 2-3 years, only to never have that timeline move forward. Ask them 6 months or a year after the engagement party, and they're still planning the wedding for "2-3 years from now." We don't want that to happen to your move!Look back to the question for "when does it feel right to get started?" when I suggested you ask yourself what feels right in your body: beginning your Franceformation in 6 months, a year, 3 years, or 5 years down the line. What felt good to you? Now, based on your answer, go to your google calendar, a "future you" app, or some kind of email reminder app, and schedule in a reminder to re-read this book in 6 months or 12 months. It's short. You can do it. And then, when you reread it and are newly inspired to Franceform your life, ask yourself those questions again and reevaluate your readiness to move.

4. Read Foolproof French Visas.

Oftentimes, one of the biggest obstacles people have to moving is that they don't know how to work out their visa and financial situation. It becomes a catch-22: they don't feel ready to invest in support for their move because they can't see how to solve their problem of finding employment, creating a business, or getting enough money to ensure they can move, but at the same time, not having the support prevents them from identifying possible solutions and opportunities. I've packed all of my knowledge about French visa types and the immigration process into a comprehensive book, entitled *Foolproof French Visas,* to help you to identify your potential path(s) to France and the requirements for each one.

You can purchase *Foolproof French Visas* here: https://payhip.com/b/KG0z.

5. Schedule a paid consultation with me to create a timeline and to get help on overcoming your obstacles to move.

You may have lots of questions about living in France, and on everything from starting a business to filing taxes to enrolling your kids in school, and you may want to get these questions answered as part of your research phase before you know you're ready to move forward with relocation assistance. If you're more than 6 months from your intended move, and you want to schedule an hour to pick my brain on anything France-related, we can set up a paid consultation where I can provide information and answer all of your questions on anything from visas to exchanging your driver's license. You get free reign during this call to ask me anything, and I can suggest employment options and places to look for jobs, or help you identify your best options for moving.

If, after answering your questions, we determine that you're more ready to move than you thought, we can schedule a free follow-up call to discuss the possibility of working together on your relocation. The amount you pay for the call will be deducted from the cost of any *Franceformation* service package you sign up for within 3 months.

Purchase a 60-minute call: https://payhip.com/b/qMDs
Purchase a 60-minute call and *Foolproof French Visas:* https://payhip.com/b/07xl

I'm Allison.

I'm a Franceformation consultant for people moving to France to help them imagine and align with their dream lives, get the right visa for creating the life they envision and navigate the French bureaucratic procedures that will enable them to achieve their goals. I work with highly motivated, creative, and heart-centered people who want to design a whole new life for themselves in France, who struggle with finding the right path for bringing their new life to life, and who would like to be fully supported as they blossom and s'épanouir into who they truly are.

What separates my service from other relocation consultants is I ONLY work with passionate people who are immigrating independently and because of this, clients receive personalized support and unbridled enthusiasm as they take their leap of faith into a new life, whether they're retiring or taking a sabbatical, seeking employment and visa sponsorship, or creating or moving a self-employment activity to France. Because my clients are fully supported from the very beginning - from figuring out the right work opportunity and visa for them, through the labyrinth of a full year of French administration, to understanding culture shock and the rollar coaster of cultural adaptation, all the way to the finish line of their first visa renewal, they can truly flourish and thrive in their new home.

In this interview, I want to introduce myself and talk about how I started Paris Unraveled in 2011 and became a Franceformation consultant helping people to achieve their goal of moving to France. I believe immigration is getting harder just as it's becoming more critical to creating a globalized, interconnected, and more empathetic world, and I'm on a mission to help make dreams bigger and the world smaller, one Franceformation at a time.

Who are you, how long have you been in France, and how did you end up here?

After studying abroad for a year in college, I completely fell in love with Paris, and I moved back the fall after I graduated. I've been in France for over 10 years, and I started out as a student in a master's program in comparative literature in a French university. I was excited to study directly in a French university, not only because it improved my French so much, but also because I paid a grand total of €452 for a year of tuition AND a year of student health insurance. The same master's (not a lucrative one, I might add!) would have cost me $40,000 in tuition if I'd stayed at Columbia.

As many Americans do, I spent the first two years teaching English with TAPIF to finance my studies. Initially, I wasn't sure if I intended to stay in France, and I was applying to PhD programs back in the US. Ultimately, I began a second master's degree to be able to stay in France, and I found a job working in an American accounting firm, where I learned all about expat taxes and tax treaties.

I ended up getting married to my French boyfriend,

enabling me to get French residency easily. But part of what pushed me to marriage, perhaps before I was ready (I was young!), was that fear of not being "good enough" to manage to stay in France on my own, of not finding the right job or the right kind of living to enable me to live my dream. While I don't regret being married, I do think that going the relationship route impacted my confidence in my ability to navigate the job and administrative challenges for myself, and it puts pressure on the relationship. And of course, if the relationship doesn't go well (I was lucky, but know people who weren't), it can create a whole set of problems for people who want to stay in France after ending a marriage.

What I want is to give people the freedom to create their dream lives in France, whatever that may look like, and to navigate the immigration process outside of the typical confines of employment sponsorship or marriage. The truth is that I believe those paths to relocation - while they seem easier - stifle creativity, limit freedom, and ultimately suffocate those who benefit from them. In choosing entrepreneurship, and in helping my clients to be fully informed about the different immigration possibilities and develop their own professional projects and career paths, I hope to empower them to embrace the true freedom that comes from creating their dream life outside of patriarchal and capitalist immigration structures and from becoming a citizen of the world.

What gave you the idea to move to France in the first place?

My aunt, a biology professor and a researcher, spent a year in Paris when I was 6. She taught me some French and told me about Paris, and I always wanted to come here. I always knew I'd study abroad in France.

In high school, after a friend died, I wanted to leave, to travel as far as possible, and I almost considered spending my senior year of high school doing an exchange program. I didn't, but moving to France, first to study abroad for a year and then to live permanently, ended up being an important part of my grieving process. It helped me to get away from everything and get back to myself: the pleasure of discovering new places, the peace from having beautiful surroundings, and the challenge of expressing my thoughts in a new language helped to heal my brain and my heart. I needed a complete change in my life to examine what I really wanted and how I could use my gifts to impact the world.

What were your biggest challenges when moving?

When I studied abroad, I had the full support of Columbia's study abroad program and its administrators, and they were available to answer lots of questions about French administration and completed a lot of the bureaucracy stuff on our behalf. When I moved independently, I was practically drowning in all of the stuff I had to do and figure out on my own. Even though I was completely fluent in French, I felt like I was constantly missing something or figuring out something important after-the-fact.

Plus, the isolation and lack of connection were very difficult. I suffered a lot from anxiety and panic attacks, and bouts of depression. But it took me a while to figure out what was going on, because I was mostly high-functioning. I was grateful for having social media and apps like Skype to stay in touch with family and friends back home for free, because I was very lonely for the first few years.

How did you start helping people move to France?

The fact that I could study independently for so little money made me wonder why other people, especially other students, weren't taking advantage of the opportunity to study abroad on their own instead of paying an American university program upwards of $40,000 for the same classes. Obviously, the American university programs provided a service helping with French administration and housing and all of that stuff that made things so much easier for their students, but there was no reason why highly motivated and intelligent individuals couldn't enroll directly in French universities instead, saving thousands. I thought I had made a really important discovery, and was excited to share it with people, so I started writing about how I did it and offering to guide other students through the process.

Initially, I wrote a book, which instead became a website, and then after a couple of years, I began offering services. When I started, it was hard to get information even from official French sites, and it was practically impossible to get information in English. Facebook groups didn't exist yet, and the internet forums that existed weren't super useful and didn't always have the right information. I really pioneered a lot of the accessible how-tos of French bureaucracy and a lot of people found my site that way.

As I added more information to my site, I began offering services, first to students who wanted to study independently as I had, and then to others who wanted to move independently and work as freelancers or remote workers. The appeal of helping clients to work on all kinds of different businesses and launch many different types of entrepreneurial projects was exciting, because I love coming up with new business ideas and brainstorming how to make them work.

Have you helped anyone like me before?
In the 6 years I've been helping people move to France - and 8 years since I began writing Paris Unraveled, I've made it my mission to make French bureaucracy as accessible and as easy to undestand as possible. I've helped all kinds of clients, from EU citizens needing help with specific administrative problems like converting a driver's license or registering for unemployment benefits, to students applying for degree programs so they could seek employment in France, to aspiring self-employed people and entrepreneurs who wanted to make their own mark on the world by leaning into service as they moved.

Each person's path to France is unique, and yet, my clients all share certain commonailities and dreams. They seek to radically shift their lives, and they need the tools not just to overcome the concrete barriers of bureaucracy, but to revolutionize their mindset so they can fully embrace their dream.

What do you look for in a client? How do I know if we'll be a good fit to work together?

I love working with people who dream big and who have lots of ideas and plans. They're not just looking for one job narrowly in one field where they've already worked for years, nor are they people who are "settling" for "just" taking French classes   - they're people who are open-minded about all of the possibilities and willing to trust the process.

Sometimes, clients come to me with a very strong vision of what they want their future life in France to look like, and those people are fun to work with because the strength of their belief makes our work exciting and invigorating. Other times, the only clear desire is the desire to come to France, and we work together to fill in the grid and to imagine the possibilities for the move. In the second case, the challenge can be in refusing to get bogged down in worrying about whether a particular idea will work. In clients who don't have a specific vision yet, we have to work to establish trust, so I can pull desires out of the client to weave the application, without them feeling like I'm imposing my vision for their future life, or choosing what is easiest for my work, and without triggering a belief that "it will never work." If the client develops reluctance or resistance while we're working together, it becomes very, very difficult to co-create anything.

Why should I work with you instead of someone else?
Other relocation professionals tend to work with large international companies and be very problem-oriented. Their client is the company moving its employee, and their objective is to anticipate and solve problems of bureaucracy as they arise. It can be a great approach, and it's one I've used occasionally, but it can set people up for failure.

Why? Because when you only address individual administrative and practical issues while ignoring the identity shift it takes to successfully transform your life through an international move, you risk being blindsided by your limiting beliefs or being held back by your fears.

What if I don't know exactly when I want to move to France?
A lot of times people resist setting a fixed departure date because they're waiting: waiting for the money to be there, waiting to find the right job, waiting to be 100% certain that things are going to work out. But the truth is, if you wait until the circumstances are perfect, you're probably never

going to move. You have to begin taking action first.

Part of what I do is help my clients get ready to get ready. They take the first step by deciding to work with me on creating their dream, and we weave it into a vision at the same time as we're working on whatever leads their visa application. Being emotionally and psychologically ready for the challenges of an international move, combined with a career or job change, and speaking in a new language, and living in a new culture, all takes time. Committing to the move without committing to the work of getting ready to get ready is nonsensical. And some of the packages take several months to put together, anyway, meaning that you'll be doing the work of getting ready as we're working together.

If you don't have a specific start date in mind, we can begin with a nonrefundable deposit to schedule in a tentative date and to get you access to the tools and materials I use to help clients acclimate to the reality of their move. We can reevaluate your plans as the date of our first meeting to work on your application approaches, and push back the start date a bit at no additional charge, while locking in the payment plan you chose, if you're truly not ready.

How do I know I'm ready to start the process and talk to you?

Each client has her own path to being ready to begin, and her own timeline for getting ready to be ready. Some clients have been working towards the idea of a move to France for months or years, and others have just begun the process. Aligning all of the elements of the move and of your energy so you can set yourself up to thrive and find a new level of personal fulfilment in your life can take time, but it can move more quickly when you have guidance from someone who is experienced with the particular blocks and challenges you're likely to face and who can help you navigate through them with ease.

The truth is that only you can know if you're ready to make the commitment and if you're willing to invest your time, energy, and money into making your move a reality. An international move isn't cheap, but the time and frustration you save by having help frees you up to focus on your dreams and imagining the life you want to create for yourself, instead of the nitty-gritty of the mundane administration that can trip you up and create resistance to what you want.

Removing the mental blocks and resistance to your dream is just as important as, if not more important than navigating the actual bureaucratic gatekeeping. When we work together, I can hold up a mirror to help you see what's holding you back. The personal transformation that will enable you to leave behind your current life and to create a new reality for yourself is well-worth it, but it will cost you the life you currently have and test what you are willing to give up.

What if I'm not able to invest in coaching for my move to France?

Having your finances in order and enough money for the visa Powers That Be is a very important part of a successful visa application - unless you're applying as the family member of a French citizen and therefore don't need to prove income and financial resources for your application. So I completely understand if investing in assistance is out of the realm of possibility at the moment.

If you truly have no money, then I want you to start by reading *Foolproof French Visas* (here: https://payhip.com/b/KG0z) to get an idea of what type of visa you'll ultimately want to apply for. Once you have a general idea of what kind of visa you'll go for and its requirements, you'll know approximately how much money you'll need to begin saving, and you can set a monthly savings goal to begin working towards your move. You can also research the amount of money you'll need for specific moving expenses, like a plane ticket from your location to France at the time of year you'll want to move, and the average cost of a small studio apartment in the area where you want to live.

You can begin saving for your move and working on envisioning exactly what you'd like to do in France. Once the move is in the realm of financial possibility, it will be easier to align you with an employment opportunity and a visa type and to determine how you specifically may benefit from personalized assistance. When you move closer to your goal, the path will become clearer.

If you have some financial resources and are questioning your readiness, I want you to carefully consider whether you're holding back on the investment because you're afraid that the move won't work out, and ask yourself a few questions:

- Are you not committing financially to your Franceformation because you're worried about paying for something that might not work out?

- Are you holding on to the money because you're worried that you might not get more quickly enough, and then you might not have enough for the visa application and relocation expenses themselves?

- Do you feel like you have to struggle and do everything yourself to fully "deserve" this major life change? Do you feel like it's somehow cheating or making it too easy to have someone guiding you through the process?

- Are there other areas in your life, or is it a pattern for you, that you won't fully commit until the results are guaranteed and you know exactly how things are going to turn out?

It's okay if you're not ready. And it's okay if you're getting ready to be ready. Financial constraints can be very real, but if you're going to commit to completely changing your life, you owe it to yourself. Let it take as long as it takes, but denying yourself the support you'll need to ensure your success is only going to prolong the struggle.

BONUS CHAPTER: Visa FAQ

To help you understand a few of the most important aspects of the visa process, I have included a couple of the most significant frequently asked questions about visas. Of course, all of this information is covered far more in-depth in _Foolproof French Visas_.

Do I need a visa before I go? Can I apply sur place (once in France)?

If you want to stay for more than 90 days in France and are NOT an EU citizen, you MUST apply for one of the long-stay visa types before you leave. If not, you will have to return to the US (or your home country) before the end of 90 days to apply for the visa.

Two important exceptions:

1) If you are the spouse of an EU citizen who is NOT French, you MUST apply for your carte de séjour directly in France, and you cannot apply for a visa before leaving. To do this, you must be able to prove that your spouse is exercising his/her EU treaty rights. You can read more about that in _Foolproof French Visas_. If you would like to work right away upon arriving in France, I recommend applying for a different visa type before departure.

2) If you are the spouse of a French citizen, you can theoretically apply for a carte de séjour after being married in France and living together for more than 3 months. You will have to pay a taxe de régularisation. HOWEVER, you will have to prove 3 months of residence in France before you can make your appointment, and it will take several months to receive an appointment and carte de séjour after your initial meeting at the préfecture. During this time, you will be unable to work until your carte de séjour is approved. If finances are tight and you don't want to be unemployed for several months, I highly recommend applying for a visa in your home country, which will be faster and more efficient than applying directly in France.

What type of visa should I get?
If you haven't already, you should read Foolproof French Visas (purchase here: https://payhip.com/b/KG0z) to understand all of the different options for moving to France and to determine the type of visa that best suits your needs.

If there are multiple visa types that potentially appeal to you or you're not sure exactly which one will be most appropriate, we can keep the possibilities open while working together and target employment opportunities or other projects that may qualify you for more than one visa category. The visa type we ultimately submit an application for will be dependant on the main money-making activity you expect to focus on during your time in France. When we begin working together, it will be based on your Franceformation Profile, and the specific visa application will come after we have settled on exactly what kind of application we're putting together.

When should I have my visa appointment?
You can have your visa appointment any time up to 90 days before you intend to depart for France. I typically recommend scheduling your visa appointment no later than 1 month before your departure date.

How do I schedule my visa appointment?
You will have to schedule your visa appointment through the VFS Global office most convenient for you. Appointment times are typically made available 6-8 weeks in advance

How long will it take me to get my visa?
Typically, my clients receive their approved visas and passports back within 10-14 calendar days of their VFS appointment. However, I advise clients to schedule their

VFS appointment no later than 1 month before their desired departure for France, and slightly more if it's a busy time of year (summer) or if there are French or American national holidays during that time (May and December). This helps to ensure you won't have to reschedule your flight if your visa is delayed.

How will having professional coaching and the *Franceformation* process help me to accelerate my move and create my dream life?

The fastest way to bring something into your reality is to focus on the end result, align your energy and actions with it, and to feel good during the process.

When you're in the struggle - figuring out what to do next, where to get the right information, and worrying about whether what you want to do is even possible, you slow down and create doubt and resistance to your goal. By having professional assistance - help envisioning the end result from someone who KNOWS what's possible and how to get there - you can focusing your energy on creating your dream because you're not scattering your energy through worry or trying to manage the unknown.

Can you guarantee I'll get my visa?

Unfortunately, I have no control over whether or not your visa is issued, and neither does any immigration consultant or attorney. Each year, over 3 million visa applications are processed by French consulates around the world, and about 300,000 - about 10% - are approved. Whether your visa is approved depends not only on the quality of your application but on mysterious factors like the number of your type of application currently being reviewed and the agent's feelings about your project's viability. My acceptance rate for visa applications is well over 95%, so I am confident that we will be able to navigate the visa process successfully, but it is never a sure thing.

With your commitment and cooperation, I promise to work with you to create a strong profile for whatever opportunity and visa type best suit your needs, and, in the case that your visa application is rejected (which has only ever happened to my clients twice!), to revise and resubmit your application one time at no additional charge.

Introduction to Foolproof French Visas

If you want to move to France, you may not know where to begin in evaluating all of the different ways to move to France, establishing which visas you could potentially apply for, or which types of international mobility programs you may be eligible for.

This book is going to provide an overview of each type of visa so you can determine the visa type most compatible with your move and understand how to apply for it. For each visa type, we'll not only cover the requirements for obtaining each visa, but also what you are and are not allowed to do on each visa type. The goal is to not only help you to choose the visa that is most appropriate for your stay in France, but also to help you create a long-term plan for staying in France if you would like, and for helping you to understand the vocabulary and administrative procedures related to your stay.

By the end of this book you should:
- ✓ Understand the different vocabulary related to the visa application and renewal process.
- ✓ Know what visa type is most appropriate for you and what documents you will need to submit to apply for it.

✓ Know the timeline of when you should begin acquiring documents and when you want to arrive in France.

✓ Understand how to maintain and renew your selected visa type.

✓ Understand if you will ever have to change your visa status and whether or not you will become eligible for permanent residency in France (10-year carte de résident) or naturalization as a French citizen.

✓ Know what documents you need to submit for a visa application for yourself and your family members and how to maximize your chances for success.

✓ Understand what you will need to do to renew your visa at the end of your first year, and what documents you will be required to submit for your appointment.

The Ever-Changing Regulations on French Visas
I have been in the business of helping people with French visas since I started writing Paris Unraveled in 2010, and began offering services to those moving to France in 2012. The different visa types, their regulations and requirements, and the procedures for applying and

renewing have all changed, for each visa type, roughly every year and a half. Sometimes without much warning. Visa types have been eliminated (Compétences et Talents) and reconfigured (Passeport Talents).

I would therefore STRONGLY caution you against taking advice from random people on the internet who have experience only with their own visa, or who applied longer than 1 year ago. You should also consider whether the people offering advice submitted their application at the same consulate or VFS office as you will, or at the same préfecture. While the standards and general guidelines are the same, the *application* of those guidelines by thousands of people across hundreds of offices in France and around the world can be vastly different. Even factors like nationality, and quotas, and the time of year you apply can have an impact on your file and its processing time, outside of the overall quality of your application.

Taking advice from non-professionals who are not invested in the outcome of something as important as your visa application and who do not remain informed of updates to legislation and visa application and renewal procedures can potentially jeopardize the success of your application. Proceed with caution if you are getting free advice on Facebook rather than professional advice from someone who deals regularly with multiple préfectures, consulates, and visa types.

Who (what nationalities) is this book for?

The guidance in this book can be used for successful visa applications in almost all countries. With that in mind, it's important to know that there are several countries that have special bilateral agreements with France, which means that those countries may have 1) special visa requirements or 2) quotas on the number of visas granted. These special agreements primarily concern former French colonies, especially countries in North or West Africa. Before choosing a visa type, you should verify that your home country does not have special requirements or agreements that limit your visa options.

For people from countries without special bilateral agreements with France, the rules about visas and how to apply are pretty much always the same; however, the choice about whether to award a visa or not to an individual, and how many visas to award to nationals of each country, and when, is always a political choice. It is one that individual consulates or consular officials may not have a lot of control over. For this reason, applicants from countries like the United States, Australia, or Canada may have a very easy time getting a visa approved for France. The French Foreign Ministry opts to give more visas to nationals from those countries because many French citizens also want to go to those countries to live and work. Citizens from countries that have a more lopsided exchange with France may have a more difficult time getting visas, as lower numbers of visas are granted to people from some nations. Many highly qualified Indian citizens, for example, seek visas and residency permits to work in STEM fields, and a fraction of those who are qualified actually obtain their visas successfully.

This book will therefore be most useful to people from countries that do NOT have a special agreement with France. Nationals or permanent residents of the United States, Canada, Australia, New Zealand, and the United Kingdom (if Brexit happens) will benefit particularly from the contents of this book and its explanations. Nationals from other countries in North America, Asia, or non-French-speaking African countries may also benefit from its guidance.

Link to purchase: https://payhip.com/b/KG0z

www.ingramcontent.com/pod-product-compliance
Lightning Source LLC
Chambersburg PA
CBHW031300130726
47988CB00007B/2658